Mac

By James Gracie

PUBLISHING

WRITING *to* REMEMBER

79 Main Street, Newtongrange,
Midlothian EH22 4NA
Tel: 0131 344 0414   Fax: 0845 075 6085
E-mail: info@lang-syne.co.uk
www.langsyneshop.co.uk

Design by Dorothy Meikle
Printed by Printwell Ltd
© Lang Syne Publishers Ltd 2019

All rights reserved. No part of this publication may be reproduced, stored or introduced into a retrieval system, or transmitted in any form or by any means (electronic, mechanical, photocopying, recording or otherwise) without the prior written permission of Lang Syne Publishers Ltd.

ISBN 978-1-85217-075-2

MacLachlan

SEPT NAMES INCLUDE:
Ewan
Ewing
Gilchrist
Lachlan
MacEwan
MacLaughlin

MacLachlan

MOTTO:
Brave and faithful.

CREST:
Out of a crest coronet a triple towered castle.

PLANT BADGE:
Mountain Ash.

TERRITORY:
South Argyll.

Chapter one:

The origins of the clan system

by Rennie McOwan

The original Scottish clans of the Highlands and the great families of the Lowlands and Borders were gatherings of families, relatives, allies and neighbours for mutual protection against rivals or invaders.

Scotland experienced invasion from the Vikings, the Romans and English armies from the south. The Norman invasion of what is now England also had an influence on land-holding in Scotland. Some of these invaders stayed on and in time became 'Scottish'.

The word clan derives from the Gaelic language term 'clann', meaning children, and it was first used many centuries ago as communities were formed around tribal lands in glens and mountain fastnesses.

The format of clans changed over the centuries, but at its best the chief and his family held the land on behalf of all, like trustees, and the ordinary clansmen and women believed they had a blood relationship with the founder of their clan.

There were two way duties and obligations. An inadequate chief could be deposed and replaced by someone of greater ability.

Clan people had an immense pride in race. Their relationship with the chief was like adult children to a father and they had a real dignity.

The concept of clanship is very old and a more feudal notion of authority gradually crept in.

Pictland, for instance, was divided into seven principalities ruled by feudal leaders who were the strongest and most charismatic leaders of their particular groups.

By the sixth century the 'British' kingdoms of Strathclyde, Lothian and Celtic Dalriada (Argyll) had emerged and Scotland, as one nation, began to take shape in the time of King Kenneth MacAlpin.

Some chiefs claimed descent from

ancient kings which may not have been accurate in every case.

By the twelfth and thirteenth centuries the clans and families were more strongly brought under the central control of Scottish monarchs.

Lands were awarded and administered more and more under royal favour, yet the power of the area clan chiefs was still very great.

The long wars to ensure Scotland's independence against the expansionist ideas of English monarchs extended the influence of some clans and reduced the lands of others.

Those who supported Scotland's greatest king, Robert the Bruce, were awarded the territories of the families who had opposed his claim to the Scottish throne.

In the Scottish Borders country – the notorious Debatable Lands – the great families built up a ferocious reputation for providing warlike men accustomed to raiding into England and occasionally fighting one another.

Chiefs had the power to dispense justice and to confiscate lands and clan warfare produced a society where martial virtues – courage, hardiness, tenacity – were greatly admired.

Gradually the relationship between the clans and the Crown became strained as Scottish monarchs became more orientated to life in the Lowlands and, on occasion, towards England.

The Highland clans spoke a different language, Gaelic, whereas the language of Lowland Scotland and the court was Scots and in more modern times, English.

Highlanders dressed differently, had different customs, and their wild mountain land sometimes seemed almost foreign to people living in the Lowlands.

It must be emphasised that Gaelic culture was very rich and story-telling, poetry, piping, the clarsach (harp) and other music all flourished and were greatly respected.

Highland culture was different from other parts of Scotland but it was not inferior or less sophisticated.

Central Government, whether in London or Edinburgh, sometimes saw the Gaelic clans as

MacLachlan 9

"The spirit of the clan means much to thousands of people"

a challenge to their authority and some sent expeditions into the Highlands and west to crush the power of the Lords of the Isles.

Nevertheless, when the eighteenth century Jacobite Risings came along the cause of the Stuarts was mainly supported by Highland clans.

The word Jacobite comes from the Latin for James – Jacobus. The Jacobites wanted to restore the exiled Stuarts to the throne of Britain.

The monarchies of Scotland and England became one in 1603 when King James VI of Scotland (1st of England) gained the English throne after Queen Elizabeth died.

The Union of Parliaments of Scotland and England, the Treaty of Union, took place in 1707.

Some Highland clans, of course, and Lowland families opposed the Jacobites and supported the incoming Hanoverians.

After the Jacobite cause finally went down at Culloden in 1746 a kind of ethnic cleansing took place. The power of the chiefs was curtailed. Tartan and the pipes were banned in law.

Many emigrated, some because they

wanted to, some because they were evicted by force. In addition, many Highlanders left for the cities of the south to seek work.

Many of the clan lands became home to sheep and deer shooting estates.

But the warlike traditions of the clans and the great Lowland and Border families lived on, with their descendants fighting bravely for freedom in two world wars.

Remember the men from whence you came, says the Gaelic proverb, and to that could be added the role of many heroic women.

The spirit of the clan, of having roots, whether Highland or Lowland, means much to thousands of people.

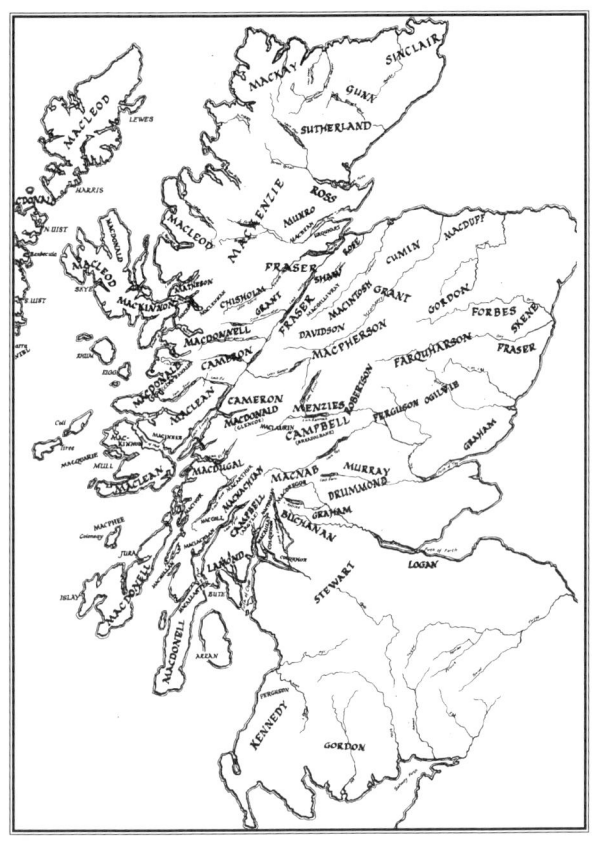

A map of the clans' homelands

Chapter two:

Scottish Chiefs and Irish Kings

The MacLachlans are supposed to be descended from Lachlan Mor ("Great Lachlan"), a powerful chieftain who lived on the shores of Loch Fyne in Argyllshire in the 13th century.

The name is encountered even before this in Ireland, however, Lochlainn was a favourite forename in a branch of the powerful Ui'neill ("O'neill") family, which was descended from the 5th century Irish king, Niall of the Nine Hostages.

The first chief of this branch was Lochlainn. The name is in fact Norse, and it may be that while Lochlainn's father was Irish, his mother was a Norse princess.

This Lochlainn and his family were forever quarrelling with the main branch of the Ui'neills as to who should be the rightful king of

Ulster. The dispute lasted well into the 13th century, when King Brian Ui'neill eventually slew Donald Maclochlainn, one of Lochlainn's descendants, in battle.

The Ui'neills are said to be the oldest traceable family in Europe, so the Maclachlans, being descended from them, have a history going back to the pagan High Kings of Tara in the 5th century.

The traditional Maclachlan territory is in Argyllshire, around Lachlan Bay and Strathlachlan on the eastern shores of Loch Fyne. Today, it's quite a small area, extending to about eleven miles long by about a mile and a half wide.

However, in earlier times, the Maclachlan lands were more extensive. They even stretched to the opposite shore of the loch, close to where the Campbells had their stronghold at Inveraray.

All this is within what was the ancient Scots kingdom of Dalraida, settled by immigrants from Ulster in the fifth and sixth centuries.

In an old genealogical manuscript,

Lachlan Mor's family tree is given as "son of Gilpatrick, son of Gilchrist, son of Aedh, son of Anrothan".

This Anrothan was a historical character. He was the cousin of Aodh Ui'neill, king of Ulster from 1030-1033.

He eventually crossed to Scotland and married a daughter of the King of Dalriada, and received lands. He is credited with being an ancestor, not only of the Maclachlans, but of the Lamonts, the Macneills of Barra, Gigha and Colonsay, the Lyons of Glamis, the Macewens, the Macswins, the Macsweeneys of Donegal and the Macsorleys.

In 1238, we find the name of Lachlan Mor's father, Gilpatrick mac Gilchrist, attached as witness to a charter in which his cousin Sir Ladman (of Clan Lamont) gave various churches in Argyll to Paisley Abbey.

By tradition, Lachlan's mother was said to have been Elizabeth, daughter of a Lord of Cowan, and therefore a member of Clan Lamont. When she married Gilpatrick, she brought as a dowry the lands that later became the Maclachlan territories.

Lachlan Mor must have been a man of independent mind. When Alexander II subdued Argyll in 1249, he demanded tribute from all the local chiefs "by the fastest messenger".

Lachlan therefore tied bags of money to the horns of a roebuck and sent it on its way to the king. That's why roebucks support the Maclachlan coat-of-arms to this day.

Because their lands were on the shores of Loch Fyne, the Maclachlans were also seafarers. You'll find, in the third quarter in this coat-of-arms, a royal galley of the kind used by the Lords of the Isles.

By 1292 the clan chief was Gileskil Maclachlan. In that year, his lands – along with those of eleven other chiefs – were brought into a newly-created Sheriffdom of Argyll by King John Baliol.

Gileskil is more commonly written as Gillescop, which translates into English as Archibald, "follower of the bishop".

MacLachlan 17

We encounter another Maclachlan in 1296, when Ewen Maclachlan was obliged to swear fealty to Edward I of England. Ewen's son Gillescop, however, was an active supporter of Bruce, and a member of his first Parliament in 1308.

In a charter dated 1314 and signed at "Castellachlan", we find this same Gillescop granting the preaching friars of Glasgow a yearly income of "forty shillings sterling" from his farmlands in Argyll.

Fighting at sea and on the land

The MacLachlan wedding feast

Many early members of the clan had an association with the church. It is said that the Maclachlans took part in the Crusades, and that many members of cadet branches entered the priesthood.

In a charter of 1436, Iain Machlachlan, "Lord of Strathlachlan", granted to his cousin Allan Maclachlan the office of *thiossachdeowra* ("crowner" or "coroner") for the lands of Glassary. This Allan was the progenitor of a cadet branch of the family known as the Maclachlans of Dunadd.

Thereafter, the Maclachlan name crops up in many official documents and charters.

By this time, the Campbells were the most powerful Argyllshire family, and the Machlachlan formed close ties with them.

In the 15th century, the then chief, Iain Maclachlan was one of the many Maclachlans to marry a Campbell heiress.

He was luckier than the first Maclachlan to do so. On that occasion, the good "brounie" who looked after the family's fortunes was so annoyed that he made the wedding feast disappear from Castle Lachlan.

In 1536, Archibald Maclachlan of that Ilk is named as one of the Earl of Argyll's 200 kin and followers who attended the wedding of James V and Princess Madeleine de Valois, daughter of Francis I of France, at Notre Dame Cathedral.

There have been some unsavoury moments in the history of the Maclachlans, however. In 1646, during the Civil War, the Campbells embarked on a massacre of the Lamonts. One of the chief instigators was the Rev. Colin Machlachlan, and because of him, many men, women and children were butchered. Someone later called him a "criminal lunatic".

The Maclachlans at this time supported the Roundheads, and in 1656 "Lauchlane MacLauchlane of the same" was appointed Justice of the Peace for Argyllshire by Oliver Cromwell.

MacLachlan 21

Chapter three:

Following Charlie

By the end of the 17th century, however, the Maclachlans were fervid Jacobites. They are said to have fought alongside Bonnie Dundee at Killiecrankie in 1689.

At the Battle of Sherrifmuir on November 13, 1715, Lachlan Maclachlan of that Ilk, the 16th chief, was a colonel in the Earl of Mar's Jacobite army.

The Earl of Argyll – head of Clan Campbell and Machlachlan's neighbour across Loch Fyne – commanded the government troops at Sherrifmuir.

Some Campbells detested Maclachlan's Jacobite sympathies, and it is said that a Campbell of Ardkinglass stalked him for five years, finally shooting him dead on September 23 1719.

Later in 1715, Lachlan was at Peterhead when James Stuart, the Old Pretender arrived on

Charge at the battle of Sherrifmuir

December 22, and he put his name to the Address of Welcome.

In the 1745 Rising, the Maclachlans once more supported the Jacobite cause, this time under their 16th chief, again called Lachlan.

Lachlan took a commission in the Young Pretender's army, and went with him on his advance into England. On reaching Carlisle, the Prince was alarmed at the lack of English recruits, and Maclachlan was sent north to Perth to seek 3000 reinforcements. He was unsuccessful.

At Culloden in 1746, he headed a force of 297 men, made up of 155 Maclachlans and 182 Macleans who placed themselves under his command, as their chief took no part in the battle.

This force was assembled between the Macintoshes and the Stewarts of Appin, and was one of the last to receive orders to charge.

As Maclachlan was advancing on horseback at the head of his regiment, he was shot by a single cannonball and killed.

The details of his death were given in a letter to Bishop Forbes in 1748 by an

Episcopalian minister, the Rev. John Maclachlan of Kilchoan.

John had been chaplain to all the clans in the Young Pretender's army, and had been in attendance at most of the battles from Prestonpans to Culloden.

He concludes his letter by saying that he now lives "like a hermit", because his parishioners were almost all killed in battle, scattered abroad, or cowed at home.

One of the Jacobites taken captive at Culloden was Major Alexander Maclachlan of Ladhill. Along with other captives he was imprisoned in Inverness under appalling conditions.

He was kept handcuffed along with other officers, and so tight were the iron bands that they eventually broke the skin of the wrists, burying themselves deep in the flesh until they disappeared. Each prisoner was half-naked, even though the weather was bitter, and was eventually allowed half a pound of uncooked oatmeal a day as a food ration.

Many died of course, but the bodies were not removed from the prison quarters, so that the living had to lie with the dead.

News of the defeat at Culloden eventually reached the Maclachlan lands – but in a tragic way. Stragglers from the fighting came back by way of Inveraray, on the west shore of Loch Fyne.

When they reached a point opposite Strathlachlan, the dead chief's horse plunged into the water and swam across. As it struggled ashore riderless, all the Maclachlans knew that their chief had been killed, and that the Jacobite cause had been lost.

As punishment for his part in the Rising, the clan chief's home – Castle Lachlan – was bombarded by a government boat until it became a ruin.

Lachlan's horse refused to leave it, however, and eventually took up residence in the rubble-strewn cellars. It remained there until it died.

Everyone assumed that the Maclachlan lands would be forfeited to the Crown, but this was not the case. The late Lachlan Maclachlan had conveyed them to his son ten years previously, so they remained within the family.

On February 12 1747, due to the intercession of the Campbell chief – no longer Earl of Argyll, but Duke – Lachlan's grandson Robert was granted a fresh charter to them.

This was a magnanimous gesture on the part of the Duke, as he had fought on the Government side during the Rising. Not only that, he did it in the face of fierce opposition from those in power in London.

But he had always been a good neighbour to the Maclachlans, even if some of the cadet branches of the family viewed them with distaste.

Chapter four:

The MacLachlans today

The castle still lies in ruins to this day, and it was not until the end of the 18th and beginning of the 19th centuries that a new one was built nearby. This was the end of the Maclachlans as significant figures in Scottish history.

Over the years, many cadet branches of the family established themselves throughout Scotland. In Argyllshire there were the Maclachlans of Craiginterve and Inchconnell.

In Stirlingshire there were the Machlachlans of Auchintroig, and in Lochaber the Maclachlans of Coruanan.

The Coruanan family was the senior cadet branch, and had the honour to be hereditary standard bearers to the Camerons of Lochiel.

Today there are clan members all over the world. Not all can claim direct descent from Lachlan Mor, however. His early followers back in the 13th century would have assumed the name mac Lachlan ("son of Lachlan") to signify that they belonged to his tribe rather than that they were of his blood.

It also signified that they had placed themselves under his protection, and that in turn they would serve and fight for him.

The largest single group of Maclachlans in the world today is to be found at Tracadie in New Brunswick, Canada. They claim descent from a Charles Maclachlan who was granted land there in 1786. The most unusual thing about them is the fact that French-Canadian is their first language.

In 1832 Lachlan Maclachlan, son of a younger brother of the chief, was elected Member of Parliament for Galway in Ireland.

However, his time there was short-lived. The following year he stood down when several of the people who had voted for him were struck off the voters' roll.

There had also been a Maclachlan in the American Congress. He was James Maclachlan, born at Ardrisaig in 1852, and he represented Los Angeles.

Nowadays there are many spellings of the name. Apart from Maclachlan, you find Maclaughlin, Maclachlin, Maclachlen and many more.

But they are all members one of the oldest clans in Scotland, which can trace its history back to 5th century Ireland.

30   *Highland weapons*

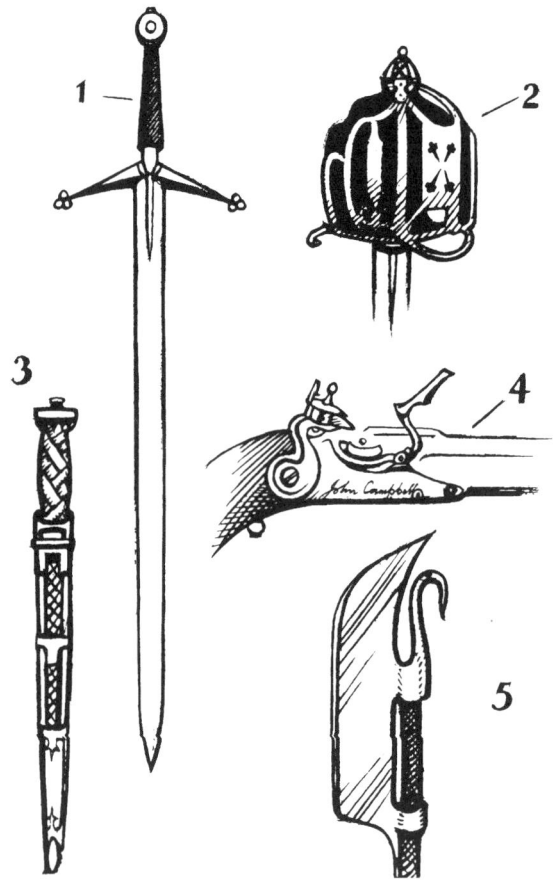

Highland weapons

1) The claymore or two-handed sword
   (fifteenth or early sixteenth century)

2) Basket hilt of broadsword
   made in Stirling, 1716

3) Highland dirk
   (eighteenth century)

4) Steel pistol *(detail)* made in Doune

5) Head of Lochaber Axe as carried
   in the '45 and earlier

GATHERING OF THE CLANS

CLAN MEMORABILIA FROM LANG SYNE

Books, postcards, Teddy bears, keyrings, mugs and much more...

**Visit our website:
www.langsyneshop.co.uk**

or write to us:
Lang Syne Publishing,
79 Main Street, Newtongrange,
Midlothian EH22 4NA
Tel: 0131 344 0414   Fax: 0845 075 6085
E-mail: info@lang-syne.co.uk